BOOKS BY ROD McKUEN

POETRY

AND AUTUMN CAME
STANYAN STREET AND OTHER SORROWS
LISTEN TO THE WARM
LONESOME CITIES
IN SOMEONE'S SHADOW
CAUGHT IN THE QUIET
FIELDS OF WONDER
AND TO EACH SEASON
COME TO ME IN SILENCE
MOMENT TO MOMENT
CELEBRATIONS OF THE HEART
BEYOND THE BOARDWALK
THE SEA AROUND ME
*COMING CLOSE TO THE EARTH

COLLECTED POEMS

TWELVE YEARS OF CHRISTMAS
A MAN ALONE
WITH LOVE . . .
THE CAROLS OF CHRISTMAS
SEASONS IN THE SUN
ALONE
*THE ROD MC KUEN OMNIBUS

PROSE

FINDING MY FATHER

COLLECTED LYRICS

NEW BALLADS
PASTORALE
THE SONGS OF ROD MC KUEN
GRAND TOUR
HAND IN HAND

*PUBLISHED ONLY IN THE UNITED KINGDOM

The Sea
Around Me

ROD McKUEN

CHEVAL BOOKS

—

SIMON AND
SCHUSTER

—

NEW YORK

Published by Simon and Schuster
A Division of Gulf & Western Corporation
Simon & Schuster Building
Rockefeller Center
1230 Avenue of the Americas
New York, New York 10020
and
Cheval Books
8440 Santa Monica Blvd.
Los Angeles, California 90069

Drawings by Hy Fujita
Manufactured in the United States of America

1   2   3   4   5   6   7   8   9   10

Library of Congress Cataloging in Publication Data

McKuen, Rod.
    The sea around me.

    I.   Title.
PS3525.A264S37   811'.5'4   77-10581
ISBN 0-671-22941-9
ISBN 0-671-23079-4 (deluxe)

Tennyson was kicking up a great deal of earth by the roadside in the way he did when I stopped on a walk, pretending he had found a rabbit hole just beside me, but I barely took any notice of him, funny though he was.

Joan Fleming

771992

This book is for an unnamed ocean,
that separates me from myself.

CONTENTS

AUTHOR'S NOTE

I have thought it true and for a long time lived by John Donne's ministry that "no man is an island" and yet I do believe that for a while I have been just that—an island to myself. Separated, adrift—though not set apart, dreaming still that tanned Tarzan will swing down from some tree and rescue me or that a dozen sirens will come singing as they form a bridge from this place to the mainland (the mainland would be to be not one, but two).

I would not willingly be a sailor, leaving land too long a time. I could not live the life of some far fisherman, hip high in water every morning, dragging in the nets at night. But the ocean has always had a pull for me.

Something tugs and tugs, I've no doubt of that, something from the sea, whichever one I'm near. And when I stray too far from beachland I'm called back. What calls or carries me till I'm within the range of water once again is a mystery. I do know that the calm times, the quiet ones—not necessarily the best—have been lived out near the sea.

No man wants the hidden hand of anything to be his pilot. He should set out on some journeys with only maps of his own choosing; no compass but the one he carries in his head. Should he then sail beyond the earth's edge it will be his business only.

A year ago, I completed a book entitled The Morning of My Life. Shortly before its intended publication I withdrew it. The reasons, I suppose, are many. Most especially, on the printed page it came out more personal than I had expected. Without its publication there is a time lapse in my life.

I have tried to cure that time lapse by chronicling my life with the sea. I am not in love with any one ocean—it would be hard for me to decide whether I like the light blue water off the coast of Greece, the deep azure color found along the coast of Mexico or the blue-black water off Fire Island best. Certainly the Atlantic and Pacific are much in evidence in this book.

By no means is this my final book about the sea, but it is an introduction as well as a collection of poems that I have saved over a time that I now feel like sharing.

A year ago I published The Sea Around Me and the Hills Above *in Great Britain. Much of that material is contained here, but that was part of a trilogy and this book, now at least, is meant to stand on its own.*

ROD McKUEN
New York, July, 1977

THE SEA AROUND ME

I

Buck had dreams
of giving Jimmy Dean
his rightful place
in the book of days.
He felt that I should help him
                    if I could.
I wanted only warmness
        and a chance to be
nobody else but me,
to live my life and my life only.

I think Buck finally understood.
One day he left the safety
                    of the beach
and traveled home
        to write his book.

Long letters used to come
from Iowa and Indiana
after Buck had left.
Come here he'd say,
there are corn-fed boys
        who bicycle
by the back porch
nearly every day,
interfering with my work
but adding to it.

Come here, come here
and help me make
        some apple-jack.

I still wanted warmness
not beneath an Indiana sun
but underneath the covers
                anywhere.
I never went to Buck.
I answered
nearly every letter
with but a paragraph,
till the letters
        stopped arriving.

II

Lenny seized the winter
between his friendly teeth
and bit a chunk or two off
                just for me.
I was left to wonder
more than ten years later
    if I stopped to thank him
           for the use
of his own heartbeat
          next to mine.

Lenny left for somewhere.
I'd get second-hand reports
*he's working in a restaurant
and now he's into water sports.*

No letter came from Lenny
in a dozen years.
I often thought of him
when I was wrapped
in woolly warmness
but more when I was not.

III

Aggie filled the beach bar
Sunday after Sunday
singing *Grandma Plays The Numbers*
her voice somewhere between a purr
and the steamboat's shout.

Aggie moved the men
who moved within the bar
then she moved herself
       back into town.

I saw a postcard once
she sent to someone else
          not me.
Honey, L.A.'s freaked
       and frigid
Your mother should have
gone to Bakersfield or Fresno.

Not Aggie, no.
In Bakersfield the jukebox
            kicks back shit
Grandma Plays The Numbers
                    wouldn't go.

I had Aggie's number
but not her line to call.
If I did I might have said
it's warm out here again
            it is, it is
you should see me
I'm as brown as you.
Warmer than I was
            but not enough.

IV

Travelers on a summer beach
in nineteen fifty-seven.
How could Santa Monica
have been so close to heaven?

One by one the houses
on the beachfront disappeared
the bay became a parking lot
Lenny's old apartment razed,
Buck's big house and loft
a new communal dwelling place.

I wish I had
the number and address
of all those friends
I knew and cared about
some twenty years ago
          in Santa Monica.

I'd like to write each one
                    and say
I'm warm, I am
for ever, always.
Someone has warmed me up
                    who means it
and I won't be cold again.

I might be lying
but I'd like to say it
anyway,

I have no clues
and no addresses,
no leads on where
my old friends
        stop or play
and so I write to them
in books and journals
hoping they are reading
all the things
that I leave out.
            Not just
between the lines
but more ahead
and further back
            than that.

This book begins
as love leaves off
then goes with me
as I go on
from sea to sea
and back—alone.

Later
finally in the hills
love opens one more door.

As always
I expect this new experience
to be the lasting,
        final one.

As always
I come away
not beaten
        or beat down
but less alive
and more confused.

CALIFORNIA BEACHES

Starting Point

ONE SEA IS NOT LIKE ANY OTHER

I am always being pulled by love
not only beds and bodies
but a city here,
          a red sail there.
A beach town
or some seaport city
always opens up her arms
in welcome to me.

I am now
the product of those
                many oceans
the sea is all I know
                for sure
but I know it well.

If the sea
did not make me
                by hand
it rubbed me, rolled me
out of darkness
                into light.
For I have seen
my past and future
on the white caps
dancing out beyond
a thousand shorelines.

I have recognized
        my face
swimming in the shallows,
my body blundering
through the gray-white foam.
My life has sailed
so far out past the tide
it's now beyond
my own far-reaching reach.

The sea makes *something*
out of *nothing* every day,
by the running in
and running back
of the tide alone.

And with the aid
of but a little sand
it polishes and hones
the bottom of the world
         twice daily.

One ocean for me
is not like any other
except to say
that each has given *comfort*
        when I needed it,
love when there was none
           forthcoming
from another quarter,
peace if I stayed long enough
to wait for it or seek it out.

NEWPORT

Somewhere in Newport
there's a face I cupped
not out of love but out of need,
and that face wonders still
why I went away
after saying what I did.
Yet I'm so far beyond
the lies of Newport
I don't remember
what it was I said.

In North Beach, San Francisco,
moving deliberately and slow
a love denied to me
walks home and not alone.

I couldn't find my way
through North Beach now
or down the long Pacific coast
with the aid of lies or love.

And I am not ashamed
though sometimes I go home afraid.

I worry only
that when love does come
I might not know its smile
                for sure
or recognize its face.

So much is passed off,
praised and handed down
as love and loving
        in this life
that reality at best
must be unreal.

MORNING COLLECTION

In the half-light
we saw the swimmers
coming from the darkness
carrying the boy's body low,
as though its weight
was bending all of them
into the same submission.
As though the boy
was pulling them down now
the way the sea had pulled him
to herself.

He was of course
just one more lover
of the gray-blue water.
A muscled boy who swam
a few yards farther out
                    each day.
                    But so young.
I wonder what he said
as he went down
that final time,
here I am or *let me go?*

I know the sea eats up
the men who love her most,
the way the killer queen
must finally one day
            reject the troops
who fought for her on battlefields
and fought with her in bedrooms.

I am not afraid.
I'd go down gladly in a whirlpool
if I had ridden all day
            on a friendly wave.

But one so young
colorless, not even gasping,
too dead for even lonely.
A conscience cannot even wonder
                            why.

For the sea
it was a little murder
done with might and yet no malice.
But what a poor repayment
for a man whose only crime
was to love the wild blue water
that in a single swallow
              tore and took him.

The ocean has a lesson
for our own lives
and those we take responsibility
                          toward.
Push forward she keeps saying
till your life is bare upon the shore
until you're naked to yourself
                          and God.
Yet the Christian and the Godless
are often washed together
and broken on the rocks.

To wade the water is to learn.

You'll gain a guideline,
a seamark telling you
how far to travel.
If the sea were not
              a woman
we'd have little luck
at concentration
        and communication
and still come home in certainty
              and safety.

Morning people
tracking down the shore
retrieve the best
and see the very worst
the sea sheds on the beach.

*Hold on to me
and I'll become your enemy,
let me go and I'm your friend.*
The ocean says that every day
a thousand and a thousand times.
And every evening,
her words having pounded
in our heads all day,
we repeat them
to each other
      as our own.

So it is
that we confuse her speech
her language spoken
                wave to wave
and tide incoming
with those sentences
complex and simple
            we spit out
as dialogue invented.

The sea invents,
    we rearrange.
The sea takes out a patent,
        we infringe.
The sea holds all the rights
to all the most important works,
speaking tongues that even time
      won't modify or use.

To those of us who've listened
the sea's the only teacher
teaching, and without a copybook.

Often she demands a bitter prize,
a head to batter on the rocks
limbs to wash upon the shore
and though we wonder *why*,
is it the only question
that she leaves unanswered?

Some of us are only
treading water, hiking sand
        beach to beach
and not beyond,
pretending we're the sea's
                extension
hoping we can pass it off.
Though we seldom do
we go on trying.

Riding out the rainstorms
            when we can.
Fighting off the fog
            with friendship,
sailing through each storm
with all the confidence
of those who reel in sails
nightly and for ever,
we tread the water
        like mosquitoes.

POPCORN

Making popcorn
for the seagulls on the porch
you look up from the stove
just long enough to look away.
Some new obscurity behind your eyes
I'm not as yet at liberty to know
stays lurking there
between the popcorn and the flame.

TRANSITION

Can you guess what's wrong?
I've tried and failed
to rise above the breakers
to swift sail out the storm.
Now the chance is going
               if not gone.
Will you be the one
to start the argument tonight
or is it my turn, I forget.

I wait here for a sign,
a motion wasted on me,
proof that it is possible
for each of us to care
     for each of us.

I cannot say
how long I've waited.
Years pass by within
a single hour
to those who feel uncared for.

Had there been a sign,
I would have known.

What goes on unseen
untold to us
        by one the other
is more real
than all the sentences
our senses spoke
                and speak.

I see your face and know
a tilting of your shoulder
speaks whole paragraphs aloud
whole stories filled with proof
that what is happening
is if anything a willful lie
both of us indulge in.

This much is fact.
You do not amaze me
with your dark indifference.
You never once astound me
by being only what
          you wish to be.

I await the crumbs just now
delighted that they come
from fresh bread
        lifted out of ovens
by some hidden master baker.

No pride moves ahead
to pave my way.

I've fast become
the dark parts
        of your shadow,
little more than your extension,
hardly more than your left arm.

It tires me to know
I'm just the casing
        of a window
looking out beyond *your* world.

After I've packed up
                and gone
fly a flag
should the intruder come.

Take care to give me
fresh reports of all the ships
and all the ducks and seagulls
that sail or waddle beachward.

Be sure to tell me
if the seals come back
                this year
and how the house
gets through the winter.

Keep a diary of sorts
a notebook day to day
that I might thumb through
                or pore over
when I'm living inland
                miles away.

IF I WERE SURE OF US

If I were sure of us
I'd carry you so far away
that we'd reach seashores
                    yet unseen
and bathe in water
even fish had not yet tasted.

I am full and filled
with firm conviction sometimes
but real sureness courage comes in short supply.
Each of us can only
work at it and try.

NEGATIVE

I have carried several oceans
in my head for company
so that when I found myself
within the middle earth
I'd have water,
wide and deep enough
to wash the dirt
from every chamber
of my brain.

So assured was I
that I had water pictures
true and fixed for ever.
I came back down these dunes
towards the true sea
expecting nothing more
than what I'd thought up
                              yesterday.

But no one knows the ocean
unless they're sinking into it.
The shore is only shore
if you walk from it
to the ocean's edge and past
to be covered by its real
and not imagined wetness.
And so I cannot trust
my surest memory of you.

What did we have,
love at first
        and then some habit
an in-between, a purgatory need?
What made us come together?
            Can you say for sure?

Stay within the darkness
            and from me
just a while longer
and you'll be
only one more pond
I thought to be an ocean.
Come to me
and our collective ocean
will wash over all our days
            and troubles.

I don't believe that
but it's hard to let
so much loved
        and unlived life
go without a speech.

A pity all things started
cannot finish at the summit.
Our lack of understanding
          one the other
leaves us by the roadside
as the giant wave goes by.

The holidays
are now beginning,
decorations everywhere.
What better time
to just let go?

I'll miss our language
and the lack of it
but I would rather
walk the empty
          midnight street
than share your Christmas frown.

They say
a comet's coming
through the sky
before the Twelfth Night
                    passes.
We needn't stay here
waiting for a signal
            or a sign.
What is finished
should be finally finished
not hung on to
            like a lifeline
that has finally stretched
            and snapped.

CHRISTMAS CARD

Where do they go
the people in our lives
that sail in like green leaves
and disappear like snow?
Not just in December
or the stormy winter months
but through the year
and through the years.

Looking up a name today
I passed through three pages of G's
and found at least six names
I can't remember or never knew.

I addressed and sent
Christmas cards out and over to them
        all the same
for what if someone
            somewhere else
fingering his phone book
passed over those same names.
Happy Christmas G's and X, Y, Z's
and thank you for whatever care
or kindness you passed along to me
that my addled brain forgot.

You I remember
because of what you are
            to me.
Merry Christmas.

BIRDS

I

A band of birds,
geese I think,
flying in or back
from somewhere
to where the winter
will be less hard.

See them end to end
across the sky
hardly out of line
                by one.

Like a victory sign but wider
their formation is a marvel,
meticulous, mechanical.

And there
just above those trees
another band of birds
brings up the rear,
like a vanguard
keeping guard.

Some have landed,
and they rest
on bare-limbed trees
and telephone lines.
They dot but never blur
                    the moon.

Perched still and silent
awaiting their rotation,
strung out they spy
            in Morse code.

II

Rested, restless now
they move as one.
Picking up formation
they fly straight forward
                        overhead
blinking in the sunlight
till a better place to perch
                        is found.

I stumbled on your suitcase
                in the hallway
half an hour ago.
Have you been looking
out the window
                at the birds?

I have seen you move so often.
Set sail on so much
                    unknown sea
that I can feel the readiness
within you to be gone
but this time
I'll do all the running.
You needn't fly or migrate
                    with the birds.

Stay.
I wish you life
in great abundance
down your lifetime.
Whoever's coming,
known or unknown
on his way to you
I pray that he
will not be long
in finding you.

Don't forget
to send a postcard
telling me the news.
Did the grunion run
and did you out-distance
all the near and distant strangers,
capture them and captivate them
                    one by one?

Write me.
I'd be unhappy if I thought
that you were still out running
and had not been caught.

Tomorrow
I'll be that lone bird
winging past the morning moon
on my way below
the belt of California.

MEXICO

A House by the Sea

DOLPHINS

At midday
a school of dolphins
surface sink and zig-zag by
heading northward in the noon
then back again at sunset.

Too far out to swim to
but close enough to see
arching up and down
                amid the waves
like tumblers in a circus,
who hit the net
then bounce into the air
            and somersault again.

GECKO

The gecko's
vocal clattering
somewhere beyond
        the shutters
never seems
to get an answer.
      He clicks
at all the unexpected times
like castanets gone crazy
and without a master.

He's been here since
       the pinto morning.
Little runs he makes
then stopping to survey
a bee or fly
his long tongue
takes them by surprise
quicker and more sure
than any angler.
       Agile as an angel.

BEACH HOUSE

With the stars
all stringing out and strung
and the moon half hung
                    and hanging,
hunger starts somewhere
within my belly.
It will not be gone
with bowls of guacamole,
                    as it didn't go
with friends and family
commiserating on my loss.

I elected
to come down
to this house
and to this beach
knowing that I couldn't
leave all memory,
                    fact or fiction
in an overcoat at home.

Soon the crickets
will stop adding,
counting, summing up.

The heavy air will set all things
            to sleeping
and the steady rhythm
of this well-loved,
        well-known ocean
will conspire to keep us there.

That battle won,
another day makes ready
            to arrive,
another night to follow.

More defeats
or maybe victories
            wait ahead.
I will have to meet
and battle each alone,
but the victory party
isn't worth the having
if the celebration's done
            in solitary.

Was there rehearsal,
a time of trying out
how many starts
          and stops occurred
before the balls
fell into place?

Awhile back, I know,
but how far back
          and when?
These questions done
      and finally answered
I hope they'll not
      be asked again.

ENDLESS SUMMERS

Too much sun
within these endless summers
has made my mind forget
whose pleasure prisoner I was
when the knot was tied.
Who I pretended to
or who pretended to me
that we were living out
the lovers' dream.

Who I said words for before
should not be paramount
                or prime
only that I wrote them once.
Got them out
and out from under me,
delivered them in time
to start the chain,
broken often,
but always mended.

The most important thing I am
is a guardian of dreams,
the least important
            thing I am
                is me.

Hurry someone.
Another week and I'll be ready.

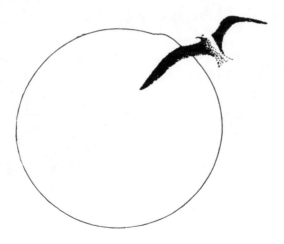

WHITEBAIT

The birds went looking
all the afternoon
for what whitebait
the fishermen had left
                    behind.
I glanced up too
half expecting some brown body
to come slowly down the sand.
What better way to waste my time
than in dreams of glory?

Many did
and many do
come down the beach.
Running, strutting,
                    sauntering,
diving in the water
sliding in the sand.
Surely one will stop
                    or look.

Take your time
brown-bodied strangers
I've more hours
than there are stones
along the coastline.

Impatience has been
                till now
an overriding trouble
        in my life
but I'll not be
        impatient any more.
The sun has calmed me,
charmed me into waiting.
I pace myself
the way the sea birds do.

Patrick's coming
in the morning
bringing brine
        and whitebait
so that we can
go out fishing too.

I do not expect
the boys of boredom
to come barging, bolting
          down the sand.
I would rather they moved
                    slowly
so that I can search them out.

I'd not wish to see
the girls of summer
parading past me
          in a pageant.
Let them file by single file
giving this one man
the chance to twice them over
not look one time, then away.

Surely
as this summer starts
there is mermaid, merman
                    somewhere
who will walk or wander by
causing me to have a cause,
a purpose for the year
                    upcoming.

If not I have
the mother ocean still
but making love to relatives
          is not as full
and all fulfilling
as being filled by strangers
          or filling up
a proper stranger's arms.

IDLE UNDER SUN

Once I thought
ideas were exceptions
            not the rule.
That is not so
they are so plentiful
that they ride by
                on air.
You've only to reach out
and snatch one
from the mist
or from nowhere.

With little raw material but sand
                the sea has made
two hundred thousand mountains
that we'll likely never know.

This being so
is it too much to ask
that each man in his lifetime
makes a single contribution,
both unique and useful,
that no man walking down the beach
has handed us before?

Why not pay back
          our birth bill
by adding an idea
          even two or six
to the many given us
without condition
          or a price?

POSTCARD HOME

Stop me I say to me;
stay my hand
should it be steady
          in its new resolve.
And yet I do believe
that like the tide
my life has come
               and gone
in circle after circle.

I've been dead
and resurrected
          many times.
Who's to say
it cannot happen yet again?

The children's noisy shrieks
are gone but stay here still
mixed with a wind just coming up
and set the sand to skipping rope
                    and dancing.

Tell those at home hello
and that I'm coming back
even if it's just to stop awhile
before I go away again.

It's raining
on the airport road
so I'll not start today,
                perhaps tomorrow,
but I'll be coming back
                before the week is out.

THE END OF JANUARY

If I knew why I had the need to travel out of my
own room, my space, to anywhere, I might be
able to explain what's gone or isn't coming.

As this out-of-season summer rolls beneath me
and away, I wait. The mystery of the sea's no
clearer than it was for me before. Worse, the
mystery of myself grows harder to discern.

I've had my fist inside the world and felt for sure
I was its axis. I've seen the kings go by, though
I'll admit my vantage point was from some dis-
tance. For derring-do I've sailed through clouds
more easily than I once floated on a pond. How-
ever jerry-built my life has been, I've felt there
was solidity of sorts. In truth there is, however
little. I built what I thought needed building—
some would say security, I'd still say solidity for
some one.

There must have been a blueprint once. Now, no trace of any master plan remains. As nobody stops or stays here still.

I do not brood. I am not malcontent. I am not. Where once I had opinions good and bad of what I'd done, even to myself, I have none now.

It, whatever that should be or is, is out there surely. I can't believe it never started, never was. I still have this life, half built—unfinished, waiting to be taken by, given to, some *one*. It was never made exclusively for me. There are takers, just that, but none that I would willingly turn my living over to. Still that's the one desire I have that overrides all others, to give, to let go of whatever I have learned, collected or amassed.

I wonder how long I can move, go through the motions, knowing what I know. How many years or days are left? Why go through the motions anyway? I don't know.

I am waiting. I will do so, while I can.

THE HILLS

HILLS AND LOWER HILLS

I sit at times as quiet as an unwound clock and hear my own heart pounding, beating, tearing up the inside of my chest. It's then that I need noise. The radio, the gramophone, the downtown street, the dogs that outside bark in harmony then unison just to break the silence.

Sometimes I do despair of love but then again it's all there, must be up ahead or anywhere. Why else would we go on, why would we continue to move forward or stand still?

I do wonder at the signposts and the neon signs announcing coming miracles. They are as sure as silver and as true as truth can be.

When I look back now I am positive the warning bell went off and yet I stumbled forward, unprepared for magic, ill prepared for you.

Hills have happened in my life. Hills and lower hills. Today I see no low hills. Everything ahead looks high and getting higher.

Too much comes and goes beneath the surface of the sea for any mind to comprehend. Will this be true as I hike hills and higher hills?

At times I feel I know the sea. At least I'm well aware of its consistency while in the midst of change. Will it take me long to know a mountainside; consider it as a familiar? Is there mystery within the mountains and do the shadows coming down at twilight make only changes on the surface or is there a depth within the hills themselves, as within a wave?

Since I seek solitude and safety from the hills now, the same or near the same as I've received from ocean after ocean, I need answers sure and true. And soon.

MEETING

I admit that I am shy.
More so with those faces
and those forms
that I start to love
with but one look only.

Back in the room
we had no liquor
          and no radio
no aphrodisiac but need.
Oh, I needed you. I did, I do.

Your bushy head
and your big eyes,
your thighs
to wrap myself around,
your intermittent smile
and stare.
Your caring for me
then and now.

I pushed a pillow
soft beneath your head
and murmured love
from the beginning.

I knew. Don't ask me how.
That we were starting
what could not be finished
            in our lifetimes.

Here we are
and those tomorrows
left or owed to me,
borrowed and as yet
            unbought for you
will not be enough.
We should move
toward the heavens
or at least above the earth
                  somewhere
            for always.

Though I know
need is not enough
      perhaps this time
simple wanting
will transcend all this
      and everything.

MIDDLE NIGHT CONFUSION

As the sun has just now
bent down into the ocean,
bend down to me.
Rising up
I promise you'll not frown.

As the stars
begin appearing
move in closer
begin to pull me
                    to you
as I pull you down.

As we roll sideways
see the path of moonlight
stretching on the water
wide enough to walk on
with an army
if one of us was God.

God is here somewhere
              between us.
I can touch and feel Him
lying up against
                  your back,
one arm extended
through the roof
exchanging bulbs
in burnt-out stars.

But wait
there is no beach at all.
No moonlight on the water
no waves sing out to me.
Can this be so,
that in these hills
away from everything
        I knew before,
the only singing
            my ears hear
is your sighs,
heavy full of thunder?

One more time
and one more time again.
You are my ocean
        and my stars,
my God and all his heaven.
And life for me begins.

Beach-bar lingo
being all the same
we were left to make
whole conversations
                with our eyes.

Add to this
that glances must be tentative
for none should know our business
                but ourselves.

I wonder then
that we met at all.
Perhaps the language
        of the desperate
is the strongest one yet made.

How else could you explain
an understanding without words?
A moving out the door
with no pre-arrangement?

PRISON

Leaning up against the wall
          in the half-light
I couldn't let you pass
without one final smile.

So it was
I tiredly undressed
not turning round again
till I had finished.

Three steps toward
          the door
and you had gone.

I cannot stay
within this room alone
or crawl back into bed
without your being here.

I am a prisoner
in my own jail,
for what place can I go
if I can't follow,
            be with you?

My brain and stomach
both are empty.
My insides drain
as each hour passes
outside your eyes
            and company.

The only thing I know
is your full body
all else has been
erased for me.

REDWOOD CITY POEM

You asked me
what the word
before good-bye is,
I replied Hello
and it was so.

You were pulling from me
even as we met
even as we touched
            the earth
making ready to move skyward
you were heading back
            into the trees.

What kind of world
have I made
            for myself
that drives you from me
apologizing as you go?

If you had been the first
that went away unsmiling
I might have questioned you
or mumbled as to mood
                and motive
but there's a pattern here
unfolding like the same scenario
every time I open up.
                Every time.

Beyond hello, before good-bye
        there should be
a string of words
or one long paragraph
to make the ending easy.

With so little time together
how could you determine
        or even guess
it wouldn't work,
get better or move upward?
Does youth give you
        special knowledge?

That I did not meet
your expectations
makes me sorry
but I am not surprised.
Still, why did you allow me,
give me dispensation,
to involve you in my life?

BOXER

I am so amazed
at finding out
my head still reels
under even friendly blows
that I'm determined
not to let the boxer
       or the battler
come in close again.

I will not willingly go out
into the evening any more
and place myself within
that enchanted circle,
the moving staircase
       or the rain.

I should stay at home
behind the iron gates
        and rainbow glass.
Sure places I've constructed.
The disappointments yet to come
can be lived by me in private.
No one need know
if the wounds are fatal
or if I'm waiting out
                some healing time.

There is an emptiness
and it is deep.
A wound so old
that healing wouldn't work.

If I have not yet
come back around
to where I started
then I am only inches
from that now narrow
                    corridor
meant to bring me there.

I AM HEADING HOMEWARD

Arms full of promises
beds full of dreams
a head full of songs and none—
no one to hear them
at close quarters.

I am heading homeward
homeward bound am I
          traveling from
the farthest point north
          in California
to its middle and to home.

Having felt your strength
come into me
from the first long touch
to the last hand clasp
I am stronger now.

But I am weak from wanting,
tied up in knots from so much need,
wound in a ball and doubled over
from happenstance
that wouldn't,
     will not go on happening.
Stopped still am I
from your so fragile so firm hand.
You left me more a boy
     and less a man
than I might have cared to be.

Listen to me
I am finally going home
to double over and be sick
on my own ground
to weep my guts out
in my own back yard.

Leaving you was hard.
Your leaving harder.
I am going home to bear witness
to your having been with me
and some time up ahead
if I am living and still looking
I'll restock the larder
you left empty.

I am still together
heading home
          but not sure how.

Though we'll not meet again
I'll still be melding into you
and sweating,
standing next to you, unsteady,
facing you afraid for always.
Down the never-ending
middle nights
out and over all the days
that may be left to me.

Your leaving gave me
my own birthmark
like the clot inside
some feeble
and unbalanced head.
I wear it up above my heart
my own red badge of courage,
my own and only birthmark
attesting to my birth
whenever.

I am heading homeward
        let me go.
The heart grows tired,
timid and afraid sometimes.
It needs to rest
as much as any head
on aching shoulders.

If I can go on
dreaming up safe seas
                and seaweed
my mind will still stay well,
but this old heart
grown older by its own mistakes
needs resting and a resting place.

SUNDAY EVENING

I

I could see
Mount Shasta when you called,
the snow and everything.
The trees and all the wrong roads
I took getting out of town.

I could feel the chill air
we'd gone walking in
     two nights past
and both your arms about me
          later in the room.

I could see your eyes
                   so well
that I was half afraid
if I reached out
            ahead of me
I might have touched them,
                        worse
that I might not.

You were back inside my life
explaining how you hadn't gone.
We were speeding, racing
                        far ahead
beyond and into years
            that hadn't come.

Here it was
the happy ending coming up.
            The summing up.

The letters start now.
Though I'm aware
that each other's absence
make us both
read into them
more than what
        they are.

Your first letter
            came today.
So much love leapt word to word
that I reread each paragraph
sure that I had done the writing
sent the missive off to you.

Your letter came
some scribblings on paper
a document to rank
with all the freedom treaties
            yet thought up.

II

More letters on the unlined page.
A *month and we'll be home*
                     together,
three weeks even less.
I love you, said on postcards
to titillate the mailman,
my crotch and head and mind
           alike and all at once.

Give me your hand across the ocean
hold it out and I'll be there.

I die, no—I am living well
basking in your now imagined smile,
praising polaroid for pictures
showing me your blue-red grin
bringing you each night to me
          home again, home again.

When I went away
I never changed my watch.
Believe that or believe it not.
Whatever time the true time was
it was only time.

I remained convinced
          and still believing
though we stood apart
that I was part of you.

MIDDLE CALIFORNIA

And Beyond

ALTERNATIVES

I have heard there are alternatives. To what, I say. To living, a man can always die. Ah, but that's the hard way out. The easy way is to go on living. I have so much life and living that needs doing I'm surprised I ever thought of death. You've but to smile at me in morning and a new life starts. When you frown that will be my excuse to live a while longer in order that I might coax a new smile out of you.

The only alternative is to be without you. I cannot imagine that now and so no alternatives exist for me. That does not mean I'm unafraid. I would that I had left to me one safety-zone. One place that I might come to, one island I might row to should you run from me.

MIDNIGHT SAVIOR

Have you come
      to save me?
          Very well.

I'm teetering
between the earth
         and hell.
I'll gladly take salvation
over pot and pills
     and cheap red wine.
I'm grateful for your arms
but open up a little more
so that I need not love you
          out of gratitude
but only for yourself.
Let me lie against your belly
inhaling all the night air
         you let out.

Let me reach inside you
slow and easy, deliberate
so that your anatomy
will be my primer,
your sighs now heavy
my own northwest wind.
              Let me probe
a secret place
no one else
        has so far touched.

Allow me this small favor
to pull you to me from the inside,
to live inside you half of every night.
        The star-filled half.

Don't be discouraged
if I fumble or become inept.
I'll try again,
        now slower still.

Then moving to your face
your eyes will dazzle me
as our mouths match,
the insides probing
one another's insides.

Slide next to me. See,
no position is uncomfortable
            or wrong.

Such space there is between your back
and each new morning.
Such emptiness
my body and the sunlight
            cannot fill.
I'll try, I will.

Remember that you caught me
on the heels of what I thought
            was love.

MIND MINDER

A butterfly flies up
inside my head,
consuming all my early years
the memory of just yesterday,
other loves and lives
I might have known or knew.

He sits and eats away
within that place I've lived
where he now lives.

Please remember for me
all those things
that need remembering.
Let me use your head
          as mine.

I ask that you
attempt to lead me,
to carry me aloft
bend down to scoop me up,
to ferry me across my life
as you would a child
across a too deep river.
You are the end of me,
and my new beginning.

You are my brother
          and my wife.
My lover and my son.
My mother and my husband
          my teacher
and the one I long to teach.

The woman
that I dreamed of finding
the friend who never was.

You transcend gender,
eliminate September,
add another month of Sundays
to a calendar well worn.

I will be for you
            whatever works.
I will work to make you *be*,
while you eliminate
the buzzing, ringing sound
that permeates my brain
                  of late.

A butterfly
and maybe more
is buzzing in my head.
If he should eat it all away
you've head enough for both of us.

If caterpillars crawl
down through my brain
you've brain enough
to see us both through
this thing that has seized me,
seized us both at once.

ADDENDUM

Time Step

AU SUIVANT

Time does its dance again. Out of focus, out of frame. Clicking in and out time.

The circle now completes itself. I regret nothing. I expect the *next* experience will be the lasting final one.

TIME ENOUGH

Find me friendly beasts
and I'll lie down
between their legs
easy and with ease.

Show me quiet shores
and I'll run down them
endlessly and without end
till my feet have blisters
from the polished sand.

Give me time enough
and I'll unwind, unset
all the clocks and watches
in the worldly world
so that I'll have time enough
to hike down quiet shores
with friendly beasts.

Should they seek me out
I'll go forward eagerly
with the wildest of the animals,
that friendliest of all the beasts.

I fear, no, I am sure
the kindness
I've discerned as love
        is limited.

A pity
for even as I feel
the end approaching
I still hold nothing back.
I am guilty only
of some dark suspicions.

I know now space and time are coming.
Enough to give me every hour
the new-math need
for adding, multiplying and dividing
emptiness and dust and ceiling cracks.

Those friends I knew in Santa Monica
all those many years ago
had in common
          a sense of time.
Time and timing's everything.

I waited just a minute longer than I should.
Alas, a single minute lost
               is not made up.

Again, I lie here in a quandary.
Which way now?
Back towards the sea?
Hike a higher hill? Where?

Some new cracks have appeared
                    across the ceiling.
They were not there
last week or yesterday
and no new earthquake
rattled at the window
or was reported on the radio.

Have I been so busy
trying to live out
        this latest dream
that wreckers came
while I was fast asleep
to tear away the final cover?

My head is turning slowly
now unhurried like this April day.
I expect that in the year
                    yet coming
I will somewhere, if not here,
        once again sleep warm.

ROD McKUEN's *books of poetry have sold in excess of sixteen million copies in hardcover, making him the best-selling and most widely read poet of our times. In addition he is the best-selling living author writing in any hardcover medium today. His poetry is taught and studied in schools, colleges, universities and seminaries throughout the world.*

Mr. McKuen is the composer of more than fifteen hundred songs that have been translated into Spanish, French, Dutch, German, Russian, Japanese, Czechoslovakian, Chinese, Norwegian, Afrikaans and Italian, among other languages. They account for the sale of more than one hundred eighty million records. His songs include "Jean," "Love's Been Good to Me," "The Importance of the Rose," "Ally Ally, Oxen Free," and several dozen songs with the French composer Jacques Brel, including "If You Go Away," "Come Jef," "Port of Amsterdam," and "Seasons in the Sun." Both writers term their writing habits together as three distinct methods: collaboration, adaptation and translation.

Mr. McKuen's film music has twice been nominated for Motion Picture Academy Awards (The

Prime of Miss Jean Brodie *and* A Boy Named Charlie Brown). *His classical music, including symphonies, concertos, piano sonatas and his very popular* Adagio for Harp & Strings, *is performed by leading orchestras. In May 1972, the Royal Philharmonic Orchestra in London premiered his* Concerto No. 3 for Piano & Orchestra, *and a suite,* The Plains of My Country. *In 1973, the Louisville Orchestra commissioned Mr. McKuen to compose a suite for orchestra and narrator entitled* The City. *It was premiered in Louisville and Danville, Kentucky, in October 1973 and was subsequently nominated for a Pulitzer Prize in Music. He has been given a new commission by the City of Portsmouth for a symphonic work to commemorate that city's friendship with Australia. The new work will be premiered in 1977, both in Portsmouth and in Australia's new Sydney Opera House.*

His Symphony No. 3, *commissioned by the Menninger Foundation in honor of its fiftieth anniversary, was premiered in 1975 in Topeka, Kansas.*

Before becoming a best-selling author and composer, Mr. McKuen worked as a laborer, radio disc jockey and newspaper columnist, among a dozen other occupations. He spent two years in the army, during and after the Korean War.

Rod McKuen makes his home in California in a rambling Spanish house, which he shares with a menagerie of Old English sheep dogs and a dozen cats. He likes outdoor sports and driving and has recently taken up flying.

As a balloonist he has flown in the skies above the western United States and South Africa. He is the subject of a new feature-length film on ballooning entitled Rod McKuen: Flying Free.

The author has recently completed the libretto and music for a new gothic musical, The Black Eagle, and his first book of prose, Finding My Father, has just been published.

Much of the author's time is now spent working for and with his non-profit foundations, Animal Concern and BASTA. He has also been active combating Anita Bryant's political group in an attempt to ensure human rights for all people. Mr. McKuen is now working on a novel.